Excel®

For Accounting
& Finance Professionals

John Masui

Order this book online at www.trafford.com
or email orders@trafford.com

Most Trafford titles are also available at major online book retailers.

Note for Librarians: A cataloguing record for this book is available from Library
and Archives Canada at www.collectionscanada.ca/amicus/index-e.html

Printed in Victoria, BC, Canada.

ISBN: 978-1-4269-1718-9

*Our mission is to efficiently provide the world's finest, most comprehensive book publishing
service, enabling every author to experience success. To find out how to publish your book, your
way, and have it available worldwide, visit us online at www.trafford.com*

Trafford rev. 08/21/2009

www.trafford.com

North America & international
toll-free: 1 888 232 4444 (USA & Canada)
phone: 250 383 6864 • fax: 812 355 4082

Dedication & Credits

Eddie Chen, Anastasia Lee, Warren & Yvonne Jung.

Simple thanks just won't do.

Table of Contents

Table of Contents

Preface

Most Excel training books on the market today are more than five hundred pages long. This book will seem short by comparison. I minimized the length for two main reasons.

First, fewer pages = fewer trees killed. Second, I want to spare the readers from "soul-crushing" boredom.

The main purpose of this book is to provide tips and short cuts to promote efficiency and productivity. The book covers material from previous versions of Excel, as well as Excel 2007. If you are making the transition to Excel 2007, I think you will find the information presented here to be of additional value.

This book is intended primarily for finance and accounting professionals who are familiar with using Excel. The information presented, however, should be of interest to anyone who wants a quick and easy guide to getting more out of this remarkable application.

My ultimate goal is to save people time so that they can focus on more important things in life.

Additional training materials such as video clips and actual files are available at www.trufflesoft/xl4pros.com. Need more help? Trufflesoft offers instructor-led online training and limited consulting.

Chapter 1: Toolbar & Short Cuts

This chapter will help you increase your productivity with easier navigation.

Toolbars

Toolbar will reduce search time for commands and speed up tasks. By creating a customized tool bar with your favorite commands, you can launch them by a single mouse click.

While Excel 2007 has many new powerful features compared to previous versions, finding them can be a challenge. These new features, as well as the older features, are nicely tucked away. Microsoft developers apparently love playing hide-and-seek.

Steps in Excel 2007

Excel 2007 adopted a "ribbon" design concept but you can use the [Quick Access Toolbar] feature to customize the top panel.

Here are the steps:

Click the drop-down menu at the top right hand corner.

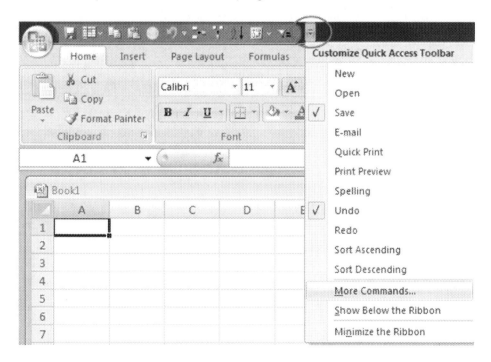

Chapter 1: Toolbar & Short Cuts

Choose "More Commands" then "Add>>" to the right-section.

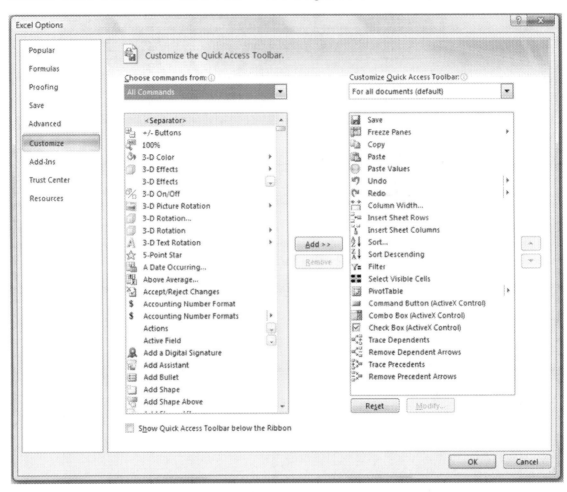

Below is my recommendation for [Quick Access Bar] customization.

- Save – Click to save.
- Freeze Panes – Header and row descriptions are kept constant.
- Copy – Click to copy.
- Paste – Click to paste.
- Paste Value – This pastes value only.
- Undo – Go back a step.
- Redo – Forward from undo.
- Column and Row – Make precise adjustment to width and height.
- Insert Row and Column – Add lines or columns.
- Sort – (1) Lowest to Highest (2) Highest to Lowest. It's important to note that if you highlight only one column – this warning will come up.
  - Expand... this option will sort the entire data set.
  - Current selection... this option sorts only the highlighted column.
- Filter – Applies auto-filter to the data set.
- Pivot Table - Slice-and-dice analysis tool.
- Select Visible Cell – Highlights "visible cells" only. "Copy" and "Paste" in this mode will paste only visible cells, which will exclude any hidden columns and rows.
- Command Button – Creates a button. You can assign a macro to a button.
- Combo Box – Manipulate value via scroll bar. Perfect for sensitivity analysis.
- Check Box – Think of an "on" and "off" switch to create scenarios.
- Trace Precedents and Remove – Create arrow(s) from cell(s) where the active cell derives its value. The "Remove" – well... it removes the arrow(s).
- Trace Dependents and Remove – Create arrow(s) to cell(s) where the active cell derives its value.

Chapter 1: Toolbar & Short Cuts

If you are using previous versions of Excel (e.g. Excel 2003), you can customize the [Toolbars] by following these steps:

Select View ==>> Toolbars ==>> Customize...

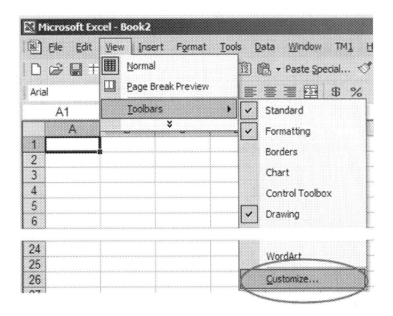

From this prompt drag the desired command icons to the toolbar. The command icons are on the right side.

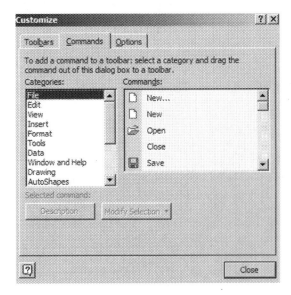

Keystroke Shortcuts

Here are some common functions that can be performed with keyboard.

Key Press	Result
Ctrl + C	Copy selected cell or area
Ctrl + X	Cut selected cell or area
Ctrl + V	Paste selected cell or area
Ctrl + S	Save file
Ctrl + F	Find
Ctrl + H	Find & replace
Ctrl + Home	Go to top left of the workbook
Ctrl + `	View formula
F2	Open cell up for editing. Also trace dependents
F9	Calculate (in manual calculation mode)
Shift + arrow key	Hold down shift key to highlight (up, down or range)
Ctrl + mouse click	Custom highlight

Copy using double-click.

Note that the cursor is a solid white cross.

	A	B	C
1	Record	Product	Status
2	R101	iPhone v2	Backlog
3	R102	iPhone v3	
4	R103	iPhone v4	
5	R104	iPhone v2	
6	R105	iPhone v3	

When you move the cursor closer to the right bottom corner it changes to a thinner cross hair.

Double click from lower right hand corner and you will copy the cell down to the last record of the adjacent populated column.

Column B ("Product"), the last record is on Line 6. That's where it will stop.

	A	B	C	
1	Record	Product	Status	
2	R101	iPhone v2	Backlog	
3	R102	iPhone v3	Backlog	
4	R103	iPhone v4	Backlog	
5	R104	iPhone v2	Backlog	
6	R105	iPhone v3	Backlog	
7				
8				

Chapter 2: Ranges and References

Use ranges and reference to personalize data tables and quickly retrieve information on demand.

Ranges

You can assign names to cells or to data tables. This technique is useful when you use features such as [index] and [Vlookup] function (covered in later chapters). Rather than typing, "A1:D20", you can name it, "data1" or give it any other useful description.

Here are the steps:

Highlight the desired cell or table range, for example, A1:D20, and then in the [Name Box] assign a name.

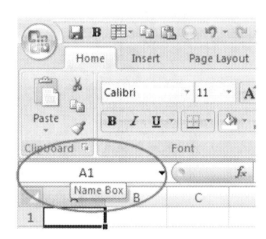

Chapter 2: Ranges and References

When you want to revise the range, you can edit the range name from: Formula tab ==>> "Name Manager" ==>> Highlight Data1 ==>> update the range in "Refers to:" box.

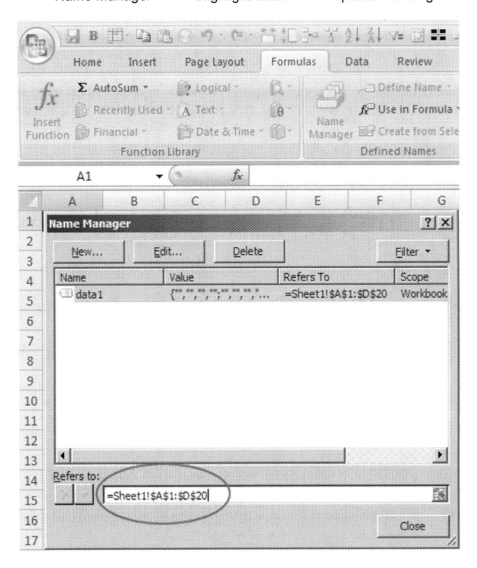

Steps in previous Excel versions

The [Name Box] feature is almost identical in previous versions of Excel.

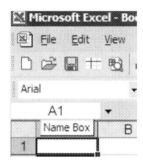

You can also set up a range through menu selection as follows: "Insert" ==>> "Name" ==>> "Define..."

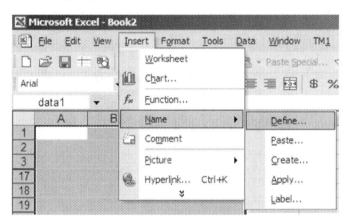

To edit go to the prompt shown below and update the range in the "Refers to:" box

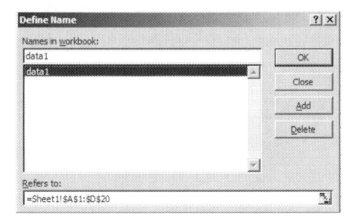

References

It's important to understand and be able to use both absolute and relative references. These features will enable you to build or replicate complex reports.

Relative reference

Here is an example of a relative reference: =A1

When you enter a relative reference, A1, and copy the cell with the formula down, the cells below it will change to A2, A3, etc. When you copy the cell with the formula across right, B1, C1, D1... will result. This is the concept behind "relative" reference since it changes relative to the original cell based on the movement.

Absolute reference

The dollar sign "$" in front of a cell designation denotes an absolute reference. You can either type "$" or press F4 (Each time you press F4 absolute reference option will change).

To indicate the column and row as absolute, use =$A$1. When you copy the cell with this reference, it will always read =$A$1, regardless of where it's copied to.

To indicate the column only is absolute, use =$A1. When you copy this reference, only the row is subject to change.

To indicate row only is absolute, use =A$1. When you copy this reference, only the column is subject to change.

Link

[Link] is a powerful tool that enables you to replicate cell reference easily. You can link a cell from a different sheet, different file, cross-directory, and even remote access instances. Note: The more complex the link, the greater the chance for errors.

Here is a sample of an external file link. Please note that when you create a link by clicking, the action automatically turns it into an absolute reference (see the previous section for the definitions of absolute versus relative references). If you want to make it a relative link, delete the "$" sign.

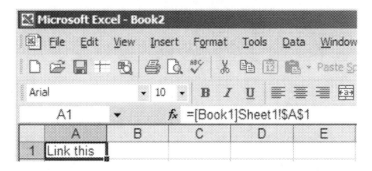

When you link a cell from a different file source, Excel will prompt you to refresh the value when you first open your file. You can manually refresh the link by going to "Data" ==>> "Edit Links" ==>> "Update Value".

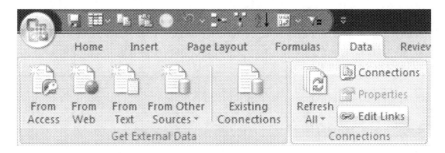

Steps in previous Excel versions

Edit ==>> Links... ==>> Update Values.

This is important to know because if you create links from files on a shared drive, where the owner of the source file make changes, you will want to be in sync.

Hyperlink

Hyperlinks do not affect formula operation. Instead, when you click on the hyperlinked cell, it will navigate to the assigned location. This is a useful feature when you have multiple tabs. For instance, I create hyperlinks in a large budget model to help navigate between main sections. This will minimize scrolling between sheets.

To create a hyperlink, place your cursor on the cell you want to link, and then right-click the mouse. This creates a pull-down menu. Then, select "Hyperlink".

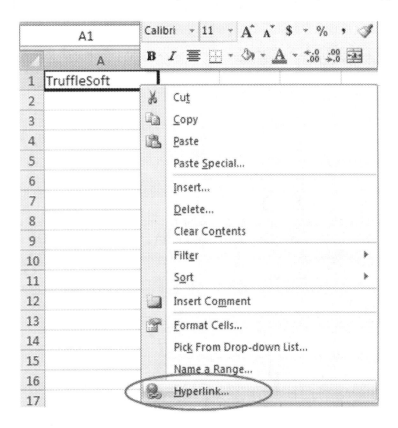

After you select "Hyperlink," you can either select the link from the directory listed, or you can manually type it in the "Address:" box.

Note: You can create either internal (your hard drive) or external (Internet-based, as shown below) hyperlinks.

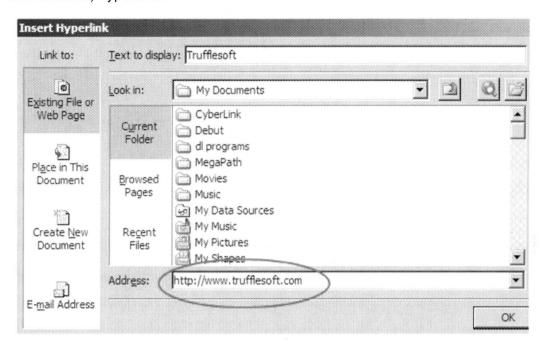

Chapter 3: Lookup

Lookup feature in Excel will help you find key records from bulky data source.

Vlookup

Arguably one of the most useful functions in Excel, [Vlookup] looks up a value from a data table. If your job requires using Excel, this function is invaluable. You can use it to build complex reports, reconcile data, fill in missing data and so on...

Syntax: =vlookup(value to lookup[1], table array[2], column index number[3], range lookup[4]).

Example 1: =VLOOKUP(A3,data,B1,FALSE)

1."Value to lookup" is WHAT to look for. In this example it is "A3" or whatever is in cell "A3".

2."Table array" is WHERE to look, which happens to be a table named "data" (remember from chapter 1 - how to create a range. The example below uses a name range called "data": A1 to G25).

3. "Column index number" is the number of columns from the matching column. This can be represented either numerically or by a cell that contains a numeric value. In this example "B1" which is 2.

4. "Range lookup" determines an exact match (False or 0) or similar match (True or 1). False will return precise matches, while True will return approximate match (this option isn't recommended due to imprecise matches). If in doubt, use "False"!

The formula can be explained as follows: Look for cell content "A3" from the table called "data" and then return a value two columns over (counting the first column).

Example 2: =VLOOKUP("R103",'sample data'!A1:G25,2,FALSE)

This formula can be explained as follows: This is slightly different way of writing the formula but it is essentially the same. Instead of a cell reference A3, you can type the actual value, "R103". Please note you need to put quotation marks for non-numeric value. The "Data" named range is replaced by 'sample data'!A1:G25. 'sample data'! refers to the ranges that are outside of the active sheet (where the formula is written).

Chapter 3: Lookup

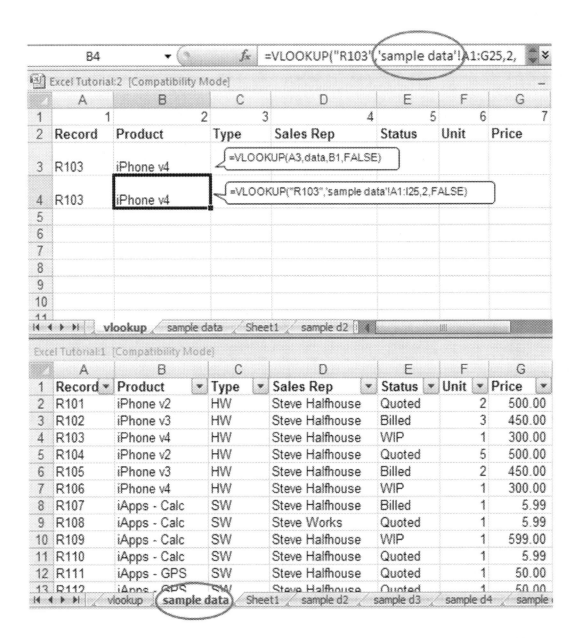

*Note: When using the "Lookup" function, it's important to note that you are working with unique records. If there are more than one R103 in the data range, [Vlookup] will return the record of first match.

Practical Application

Suppose you have two reports that you want to reconcile. "Sample data tab" is the first report and "Sample D2 tab" is the second report.

Here is how you can use the [Vlookup] function to compare the prices between the two reports. Pull in the price associated from "sample data" to "sample d2", then subtract it from "sample d2". If there is any difference between the two values, you have a variance.

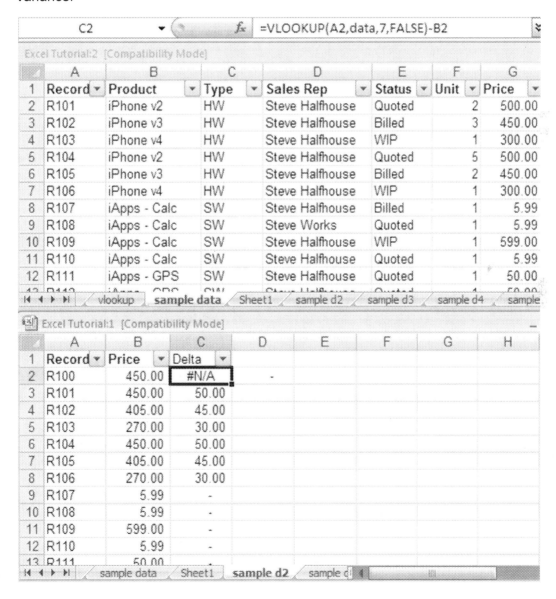

Please note that in cell C2, there is a "#N/A" error. Normally this is a nuisance, but in a reconciliation process, it is a useful error message. It's telling you that record "R100" is not found in the sample data.

In case you want to suppress #N/A error message - you will need to add in [ISNA] function:

=IF(ISNA(VLOOKUP(A2,DATA,7,FALSE)),0,VLOOKUP(A2,DATA,7,FALSE)-B2)

This formula can be explained as follows: if the value of [Vlookup] is "#N/A", then replace the value with "0" instead of "#N/A", otherwise carry out the normal [Vlookup] operation. Note: Instead of "0", you can use other values such as "value not found".

Creating a Unique Lookup Value

Suppose you have raw data that has "Month" which is not unique. However, when you concatenate the "Month" and "Type" columns, you can create a unique data column. (e.g. =B2&C2)

You can write a "Lookup" formula using the same concatenation principle. Notice that the "Lookup" value is "B18&$A18," which is same as writing "Jansw01."

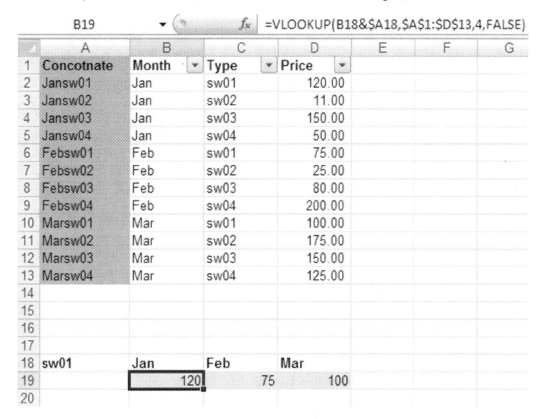

Horizontal Lookup

[HLookup] can be used for a data set that is arranged horizontally (across) rather than vertically (down), as is shown in the figure below.

C6			f_x	=HLOOKUP(B6,B1:M4,3,FALSE)		
	A	B	C	D	E	F	G
1	Month	Jan	Feb	Mar	Apr	May	Jun
2	Revenue	450	475	500	525	550	575
3	Expense	360	380	400	420	440	460
4	Profit	90	95	100	105	110	115
5							
6	Lookup	Mar	400				

Match and Index

[Match] and [Index] functions can be used where the "Lookup" value is not in the first column.

For instance, suppose you know the product name "iPhone v7" but not the record number. In that case, you can use the [Match] embedded in the [Index] function, rather than [Vlookup].

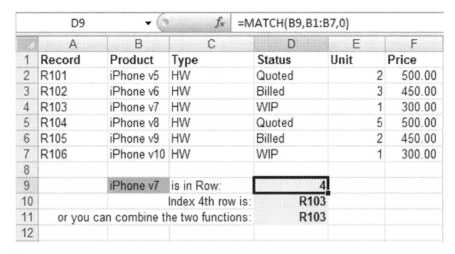

D9			f_x	=MATCH(B9,B1:B7,0)		
	A	B	C	D	E	F
1	Record	Product	Type	Status	Unit	Price
2	R101	iPhone v5	HW	Quoted	2	500.00
3	R102	iPhone v6	HW	Billed	3	450.00
4	R103	iPhone v7	HW	WIP	1	300.00
5	R104	iPhone v8	HW	Quoted	5	500.00
6	R105	iPhone v9	HW	Billed	2	450.00
7	R106	iPhone v10	HW	WIP	1	300.00
8						
9		iPhone v7	is in Row:	4		
10			Index 4th row is:	R103		
11		or you can combine the two functions:		R103		
12						

Use the match function to determine which row contains "iPhone v7". In this case, it's the fourth row down: "=MATCH(B9,B1:B7,0)"

Index value of 4 is R103 or =INDEX(A1:A7,D9,0)

Putting them together yields: =INDEX(A1:A7,MATCH(B9,B1:B7,0),0)

Chapter 4: Conditional Functions

Turn unrefined records into intelligent information.

If Statement

In the simplest terms, [If] function represents a conditional test of logic. You can use the [If] statement to build intelligence to data with various attributes (e.g. Name, Product, Period, Sale Revenue, Quota). Who sold what? When? Did the person meet quota?

Syntax: =if(condition statement, value if true, value if false)

Example 1

Cells highlighted in green (column G) contains [If] statements that check if the value in column D is equal to or greater than 6; if the answer is yes it will return "Yes", otherwise, it will return "No".

	G10			f_x	=IF(D10>=6,"Yes","No")	
	A	B	C	D	E	F	G
1	if statement						
2							
3		In a nutshell: conditional statement					
4		Syntax: =if(cell ref condition, true, false)					
5							
6							
7			Example 1: Simple if statement				
8			Table 1a				
9			Month	Value	Year		
10			Jan	1	2009		No
11			Feb	2	2009		No
12			Mar	3	2009		No
13			Apr	4	2009		No
14			May	5	2009		No
15			Jun	6	2009		Yes
16			Jul	7	2009		Yes
17			Aug	8	2009		Yes
18			Sep	9	2009		Yes
19			Oct	10	2009		Yes
20			Nov	11	2009		Yes
21			Dec	12	2009		Yes

Example 2

Here is a sample of multiple logic tests where an [If] statement is embedded within another [If] statement.

First logic: Check to see if the "Exception" column contains "NA"; if so, return a value of "NA".

Second logic: If the "Exception" does not contain "NA", then check to see if the "Actual" column is greater than or equal to "Forecast". If is, return "Yes" otherwise return "No".

G27			fx	=IF(E27="NA","NA",IF(C27>=D27,"Yes","No"))				
	B	C	D	E	F	G	H	I
24	Example 2: Multi-conditional if statement							
25	Table 2							
26	Month	Actual	Forecast	Exception				
27	Jan	5	10	NA		NA		
28	Feb	25	20			Yes		
29	Mar	10	50			No		
30	Apr	120	60			Yes		
31	May	80	100			No		
32	Jun	200	120			Yes		
33	Jul	50	200			No		
34	Aug	500	400			Yes		
35	Sep	120	500			No		
36	Oct	400	400			Yes		
37	Nov	100	150			No		
38	Dec	150	50	NA		NA		

Following this logic, you can embed a [If] statement within another [If] statement. The only limitation is the maximum number of characters allowed in a cell: 255 characters.

AND/OR Condition

[And] / [Or] can be used in conjunction with [If] to reach even more fine-tuned logic. [And] required meeting both conditions while [Or] logic requires meeting only one of the two conditions. For example, you want to see what Sales Rep Steve Halfhouse has quoted (under "Status"), below is how to use [And] inside the [If] statement.

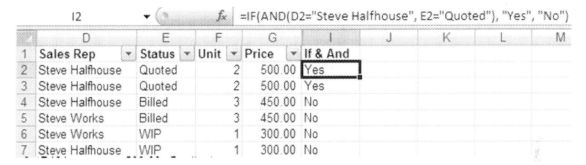

	D	E	F	G	I	J	K	L	M
1	Sales Rep	Status	Unit	Price	If & And				
2	Steve Halfhouse	Quoted	2	500.00	Yes				
3	Steve Halfhouse	Quoted	2	500.00	Yes				
4	Steve Halfhouse	Billed	3	450.00	No				
5	Steve Works	Billed	3	450.00	No				
6	Steve Works	WIP	1	300.00	No				
7	Steve Halfhouse	WIP	1	300.00	No				

Practical Application

Here is how to check for duplicate records.

Sort the data by "Record", and then use [If] to compare each of the record numbers to the one above. If you have a match then you know there are duplicate record numbers.

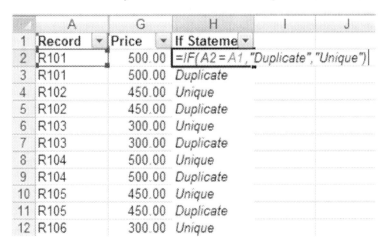

	A	G	H	I	J
1	Record	Price	If Stateme		
2	R101	500.00	=IF(A2=A1,"Duplicate","Unique")		
3	R101	500.00	Duplicate		
4	R102	450.00	Unique		
5	R102	450.00	Duplicate		
6	R103	300.00	Unique		
7	R103	300.00	Duplicate		
8	R104	500.00	Unique		
9	R104	500.00	Duplicate		
10	R105	450.00	Unique		
11	R105	450.00	Duplicate		
12	R106	300.00	Unique		

Chapter 5: Filtering

Hone in records of key interest.

Filter

The [Filter] function can be applied multiple ways to give you single-dimensional* "slice-and-dice" view of data table. While Excel 2007 introduced more enhancements over the previous versions, the filtering concept is identical and the process is very similar.

*I call it a single-dimension tool because the data table remains intact; only the lines are hidden. For a multi-dimensional analytical tool see Pivot Table in Chapter 6.

Steps in Excel 2007

Highlight the desired data range, and then apply [Filter].

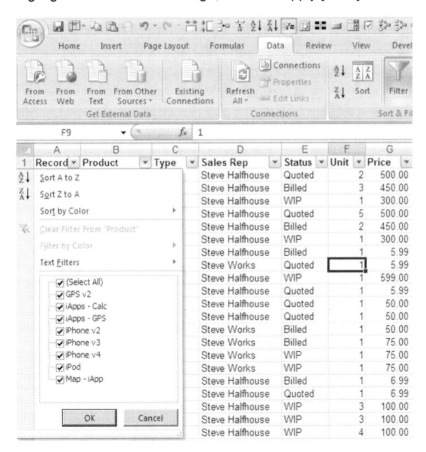

Through a system of inclusions and exclusions, you can show or hide records of interest.

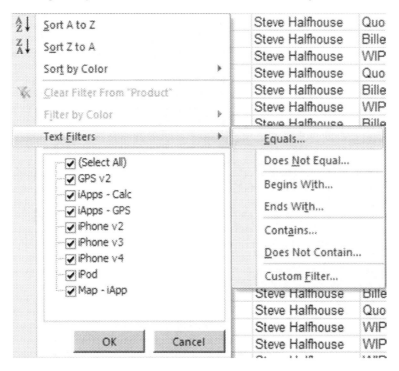

Equals...	records that equal to the value entered.
Does Not Equal...	records excluding the value entered.
Begins With...	records with match beginning value.
Ends With...	records with match ending value.
Contains...	records that contain the value entered.
Does Not Contain...	records that don't contain the value entered.

Custom Filter... You can use any of available filter options and mix them with [And] or [Or] conditions.

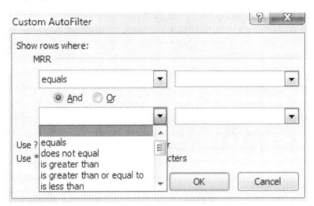

If you want to search for unique records, then go to [Advance Filters].

Select "Data" and then "Advanced Filter".

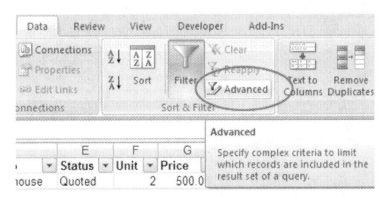

From this prompt, check the "Unique Records Only" box.

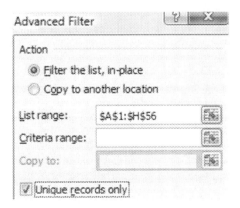

Chapter 5: Filtering

Select "Data" ==>> "Filter" ==>> "Advanced Filter..."

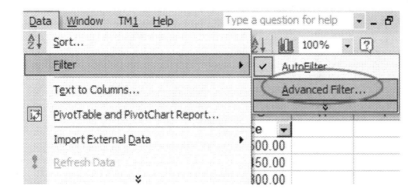

From this prompt, check the "Unique Records Only" box.

Practical Application

In an ideal world, the IT department can deliver data that you can readily use to generate a report. In the real world, this is often what you get:

	A	B	Sales
1	Type	Market	Sales
2	CABLE - Business Cable - Up To 6M x 768k Static	Small Office	Bob V
3	CABLE - Business Cable .256 Mb/.256 Mb Static	Enterprise	Bob V
4	CABLE - Business Cable .256 Mb/.256 Mb Static	Enterprise	Bob V
5	CABLE - Business Cable .256 Mb/.256 Mb Static	Enterprise	Bob V
6	CABLE - Business Cable 1.5 Mb/.768 Mb Dynamic	Small Office	Bob V
7	CABLE - Business Cable 2.0 Mb/.384 Mb	Enterprise	Bob V
8	CABLE - Business Class 256K	Enterprise	Bob V
9	CABLE - Business Class 256K	Enterprise	Bob V
10	CABLE - Business Class 256K	Enterprise	Bob V
11	CABLE - Cable - 256K	Enterprise	Bob V
12	CABLE - Cable - 256K	Enterprise	Bob V
13	CABLE - Cable Connect	Enterprise	Bob V
14	CABLE - Cable Connect	Enterprise	Bob V
15	CABLE - Cable x/.256 Mb Business	Enterprise	Bob V
16	DSL - ADSL Retail Access	Enterprise	Bob V
17	DSL - ADSL Retail Access	Enterprise	Bob V
18	DSL - ADSL Retail Access	Enterprise	Bob V
19	DSL - ADSL Retail Access	Enterprise	Bob V
20	DSL - ADSL Retail Access	Enterprise	Bob V
21	DSL - ADSL Retail Access	Enterprise	Bob V
22	DSL - ADSL Up to .768/.128 Mb Core Service Area	Enterprise	Bob V
23	DSL - ADSL Up to 1.5/.128 Mb	Enterprise	Bob V
24	DSL - ADSL Up to 1.5/.128 Mb	Enterprise	Bob V
25	DSL - ADSL Up to 1.5/.128 Mb	Enterprise	Bob V
26	DSL - ADSL up to 1.5/.128 Mb	Enterprise	Bob V
27	DSL - ADSL Up to 1.5/.128 Mbps	Enterprise	Bob V
28	DSL - ADSL Up to 1.5/.128 Mbps (3 Yr)	Enterprise	Bob V
29	DSL - ADSL Up to 1.5/.128 Mbps (3 Yr)	Enterprise	Bob V

Suppose you need to generate a report by five major product categories: ADSL, SDSL, Cable, T1 and Wireless, but the raw data above has product "type" with extraneous descriptions at the end. In addition, your problem is compounded by a data integrity issue of having wrong pricing data.

Here is what you can do:

Step 1: Create a "Product" column and apply "Filter" to all columns.

Step 2: Text filter => Contains: Type "ADSL" in the box and in column "F", type "ADSL". Repeat the process with SDSL, Cable, T1 and Wireless.

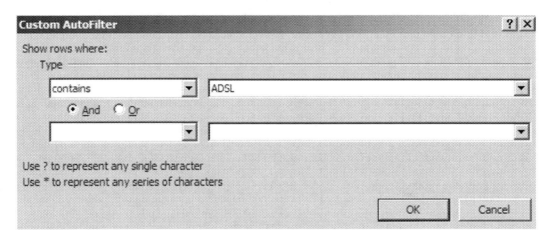

Step 3: Select "All" in "Type" and "Blank" in "Product". This action should result in the creation of a small set of data. Assign appropriate product type.

This filter will show you all the records that have "Blank" in "Product".

Step 4: Pricing issue: T1 product with revenue less than $200 is probably an error. You can check these problems by applying a filter on "Product" for T1 and another filter on "Revenue" for number filter => less than $200. This should give you all the records that are considered T1, but have revenue of less than $200.

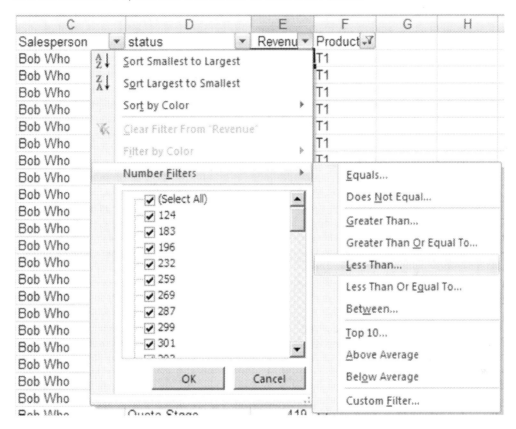

Chapter 6: Pivot Table

Pivot Table

The [Pivot table] function gives you the power to choose how the data are summarized and laid out. If [Filter] is two-dimensional, think of [Pivot table] as a multi-dimensional analytical tool.

Steps in Excel 2007

Select the data range, and then from "Insert" tab click "PivotTable".

This prompt will appear:

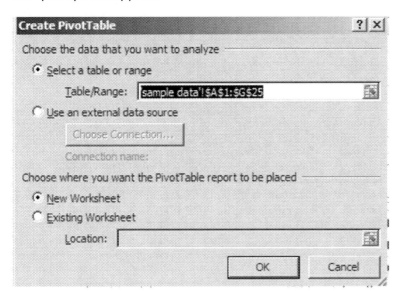

Click "OK".

Chapter 6: Pivot Table

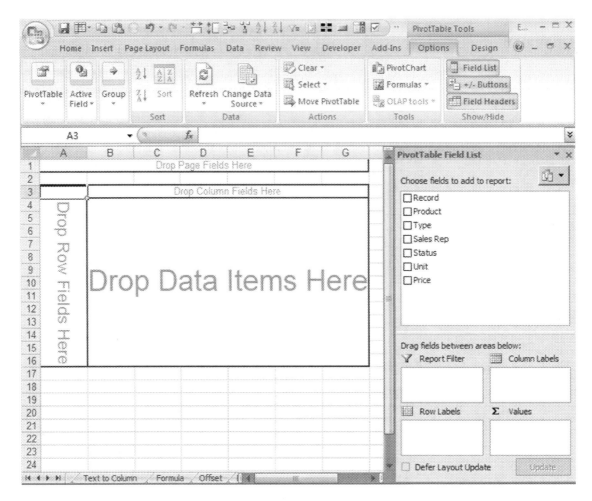

Put check-marks at "Choose field to add.." or drag and drop the fields into the "Row" or "Column" field.

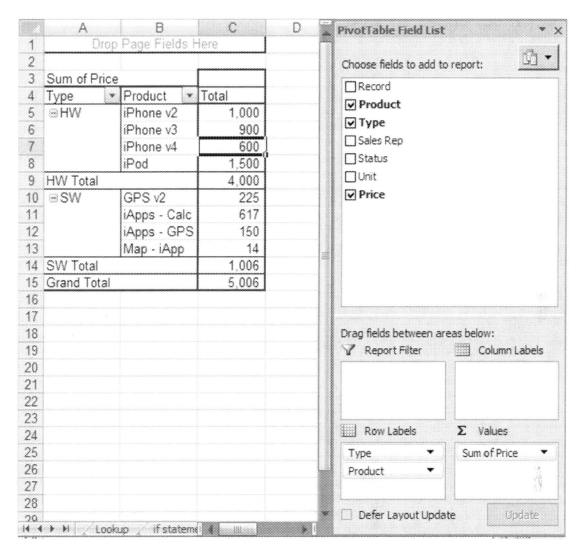

Note: If you put a non-numeric value, such as text into the "Value" field, it will result in counting of the records rather than summing.

For more examples, please check online www.trufflesoft\xl4pros.com.

Chapter 6: Pivot Table

"Data" ==>> "Pivot Table".

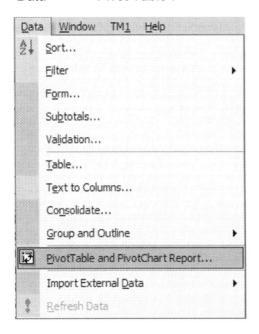

"Next" (confirm source of data).

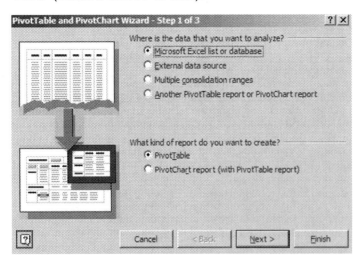

"Next" (confirm range).

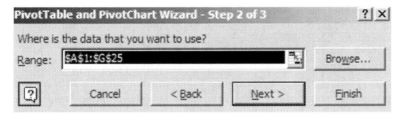

Check "New" or Existing" worksheet then press Finish.

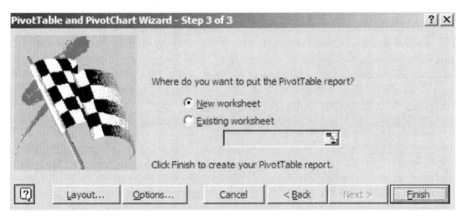

Now drag and drop the data field from the right-hand side into the appropriate space: Page, Row, Column, or Data.

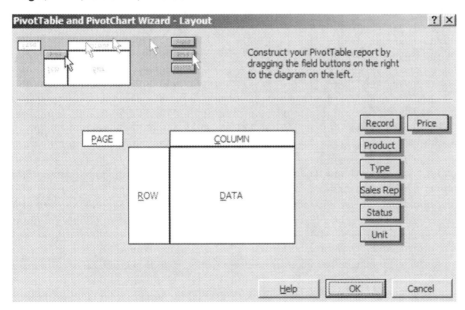

Auto fill blank section

This is a typical pivot table result.

	A	B	C
4	Type ▼	Product ▼	Total
5	⊟HW	iPhone v2	1,000
6		iPhone v3	900
7		iPhone v4	600
8		iPod	1,500
9	HW Total		4,000
10	⊟SW	GPS v2	225
11		iApps - Calc	617
12		iApps - GPS	150
13		Map - iApp	14
14	SW Total		1,006
15	Grand Total		5,006

Suppose you want to copy and paste value a [Pivot table], but you want to show all "Type" categories.

	Type	Product	Total
20	Type	Product	Total
21	HW	iPhone v2	1000
22	=A21	iPhone v3	900
23		iPhone v4	600
24		iPod	1500
25	HW Total		4000
26	SW	GPS v2	225
27		iApps - Calc	616.97
28		iApps - GPS	150
29		Map - iApp	13.98
30	SW Total		1005.95
31	Grand Total		5005.95

Create a referencing cell that is populated. In this case, "A21".

Copy cell "A21" ==>> Ctrl + G ==>> Choose "Special".

And select "Blank", this action will highlight all the blank cells.

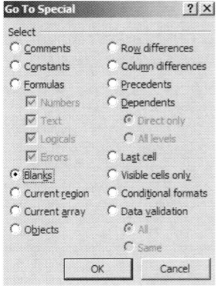

Now paste. This should be your result.

20	Type	Product	Total
21	HW	iPhone v2	1000
22	HW	iPhone v3	900
23	HW	iPhone v4	600
24	HW	iPod	1500
25	HW Total		4000
26	SW	GPS v2	225
27	SW	iApps - Calc	616.97
28	SW	iApps - GPS	150
29	SW	Map - iApp	13.98
30	SW Total	Map - iApp	1005.95
31	Grand Total		5005.95

Chapter 7: Working with text value

Systematically turn ordinary text values into more user defined values.

Text to value

Suppose your company's IT resources are limited and you are only able to get a raw data dump. What do you do with all those extraneous pieces of information that you don't need? Worse yet, the attributes you need are all crunched into a single column.

Option 1. Pick up the phone and curse at the guy responsible (not recommended).

Option 2. Use the [Text to columns] feature to parse the single column into more-useful multiple columns, and work like a pro.

Highlight column desired then go to "Data" ==>> "Text to Columns".

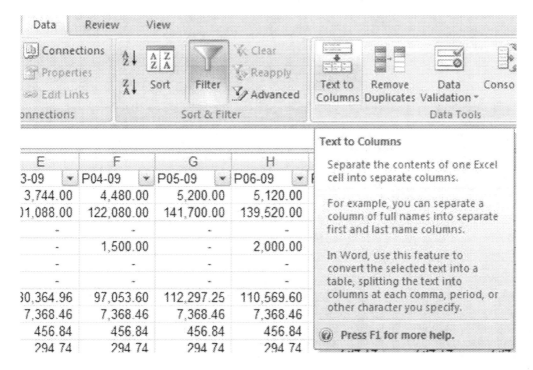

Please note that steps are identical for Excel 2007 and Previous versions of Excel.

Delimited: This option allows parsing by a specified condition or character. For example, tab, comma, or any alphanumeric character.

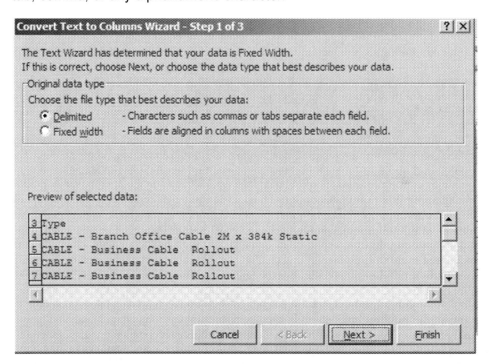

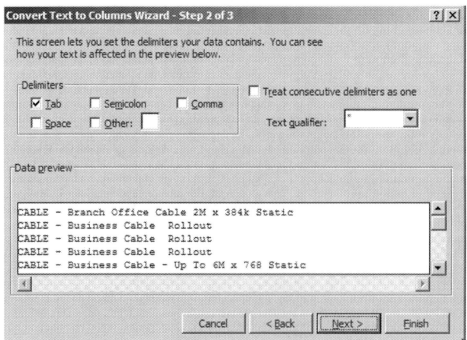

Fixed Width: Use this option for a text column that is uniform (consistent width).

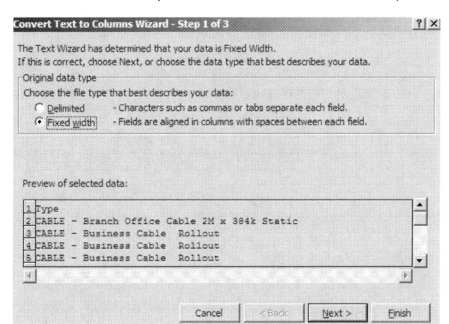

Use mouse clicks to create vertical line(s) that will divide the column(s). You can adjust the lines by moving them left or right. Double-click the line(s) to erase the line(s).

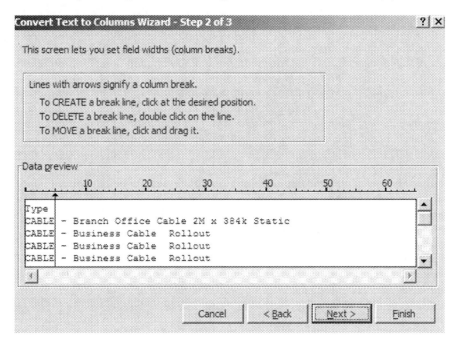

Chapter 7: Working with text value

The formulas below are commonly used in converting text values.

	A	B	C	D	E
1	**Formula**				
2					
3	_Text Formula_	Function		Formula	
4					
5	DSL - ADSL .128	Left	DSL	=LEFT(A4,3)	
6	DSL - ADSL .128	Right	128	=RIGHT(A5,3)	
7	DSL - ADSL .128	Mid	ADSL	=MID(A6,7,4)	
8	DSL - ADSL .128	Mid Find	ADSL	=MID(A8,FIND("L -",A8,1)+4,4)	

An advanced way to carve out text is to use "Find", coupled with "Left" or "Right" or "Mid". In layman's terms, this is a way to find a specific bit of text, and then start the function "Left", "Right", or "Mid". The fourth sample is how to find "L -" and then pick out "ADSL".

Chapter 8: Working with Formulas

Simplify complex tasks via advance formulas.

This chapter provides an overview of commonly used formula among accounting and financial professionals. The formula presented here will help you skip some manual calculations to get to the end results faster. Smart report equals smaller footprint.

Sumif

[Sumif] formula sums up the declared values, "Enterprise" in cell "E62".

	B79	f_x	=SUMIF(A62:A75,A78,B62:B75)		
	A	B	C	D	E
61	**Market**	**Revenue**			
62	Strategic	1,069.95			
63	Enterprise	142.00			
64	Strategic	75.00			
65	Enterprise	59.46			
66	Enterprise	86.00			
67	Enterprise	90.00			
68	SMB	90.00			
69	SMB	90.00			
70	Enterprise	90.00			
71	Enterprise	113.00			
72	Enterprise	56.00			
73	Enterprise	56.00			
74	Enterprise	56.00			
75	Enterprise	56.00			
76	Total	2,129.41			
77					
78	*Enterprise*				
79	Sum If	804.46			
80	Count If	10			
81	Count All	14			
82	Count Blank	0			

Countif

[Countif] counts the total number of declared values. There are total of ten "Enterprise" values.

=COUNTIF(A62:A75,A78)

Counta

[Counta] counts all cells that are populated (excluding blank) from lines 62 to 75. There are total of fourteen records.

=COUNTA(A62:A75)

Countblank

[Countblank] counts all blanks cells. There are no blanks so it returned zero.

=COUNTBLANK(A62:A75)

Rank

[Rank] provides the order of where the value is relative to the data range. This formula is often used for sales performance and score reporting.

The formula can be explained as follows: rank cell "A2", from "A2:A9" range, 0 (1 is ascending, 0 is descending).

SUM			f_x =RANK(A2,A$2:A$9,0)	
	A	B	C	D RANK(number, ref, [order])
1	Score	Rank		
2	90	=RANK(A2		
3	95	2		
4	85	6		
5	100	1		
6	45	8		
7	60	7		
8	95	2		
9	90	4		

Choose

[Choose] Excel chooses a value, which can be a number or text, from a series or an index based variable. In this case, B3=5 is the index and Excel chooses the fifth value in the series.

	B1	▾	f_x	5/28/2009
	A	B		C
1	Date:	39961		
2	Month:	5		=MONTH(B1)
3	Choose		May	=CHOOSE(C2,"Jan","Feb","Mar","Apr","May")
4	Date:	39905		
5	Month:	4		=MONTH(B4)
6	Choose		Apr	=CHOOSE(C5,"Jan","Feb","Mar","Apr","May")
7				

Note: Dates are stored as numeric value in Excel. You can change the cell formats to express different displays. For example 5/28/2009 is 39961.

Offset

[Offset] function lets you control how Excel handles a range of rows and/or columns based on a variable. You can automate Year-to-date (YTD) calculation, where YTD changes dynamically based any given month.

The formula can be explained as follows:

=SUM(OFFSET(B14:M14,0,0,1,$C$5))

"B14:M14": This is the reference base or starting point for the offset.

"0": This is the row reference for the offset; 0 means to stay on the same row 14; 1 means row 15.

"0": This is the column reference; 0 means to say on the base B column; 1 means C column.

"1" is the height reference; 1 means height stays on current row 14; 2 means row 14 + 15.

"$C$5": This is the width reference. In our example, this is the month variable, "2" means adding up January and February, and "5" means adding up January through May.

"Row", "Column", "Height", and "Width" can also be viewed as a dynamic square box. When you change any of these numbers, the box shifts accordingly.

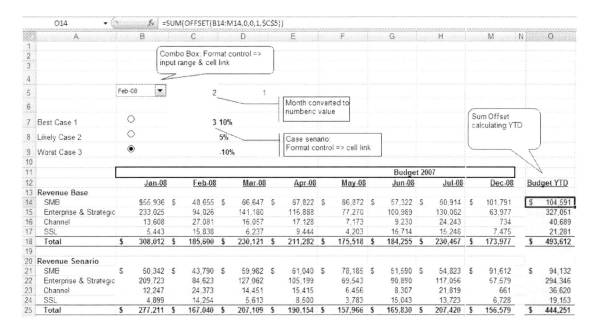

Offset illustrated in a report.

Chapter 9: Financial Calculation

IRR and MIRR

Internal rate of return (IRR) calculates cash flows based on one fixed rate, hence assuming reinvestments at the same rate. Modified internal rate of return (MIRR) assumes that all cash flows are reinvested at the firm's reinvestment rate. In cases where the cost of capital rate and the reinvestment rate differ, MIRR more accurately reflects the profitability of a project.

The example below compares IRR to MIRR.

	A13	▼	f_x	=MIRR(A2:A7,A9,A10)
	A		B	
1	Cash Flow		Description	
2	(100,000)		Initial Investment	
3	40,000		Cash flow Year 1	
4	25,000		Cash flow Year 2	
5	10,000		Cash flow Year 3	
6	50,000		Cash flow Year 4	
7	60,000		Cash flow Year 5	
8	Rates			
9	9%		Interest on initial investment	
10	10%		Interest on reinvestment	
11				
12	22%		IRR	
13	17%		MIRR	

=IRR(A2:A7,A9)

IRR will result in 22 percent.

=MIRR(A2:A7,A9,A10)

Using the firm's higher reinvestment rate will result in a lower return of 17 percent.

NPV

Net present value (NPV) – is a financial calculation that takes the difference between the costs (initial investment) and the sum of all discounted (present-day) cash flows. NPV is often used for project justification. A positive NPV means the project returns a profit.

	A	B
1	Cash Flow	Description
2	(100,000)	Initial Investment
3	40,000	Cash flow Year 1
4	25,000	Cash flow Year 2
5	10,000	Cash flow Year 3
6	50,000	Cash flow Year 4
7	60,000	Cash flow Year 5
8	Rates	
9	9%	Interest on initial investment
10	10%	Interest on reinvestment
14		
15	$185,000	Total Cash Flow
16	$32,676	NVP

Payment

Payment Calculation: This calculation is for mortgages, car loans, and other loans that involve interest rates and periodic schedules of payments.

The sample below shows how you would go about calculating a typical home loan.

Please note 10 percent is an annual rate. Therefore, you must divide the rate by 12 to convert it to a monthly rate and multiply 12 to the 30 years term in order to properly calculate the monthly payment.

A24		f_x	=PMT(A22/12,A23*12,A21)

	A	B	C
20	Home Loan		
21	$ 500,000	Loan Amount	
22	10%	Annual Mortage Rate	
23	30	Term in years	
24	($4,387.86)	Monthly Payment	

Chapter 10: Working with graphs

Create visual representation of data.

Pie Chart

As the saying goes "a picture is worth a thousand words." Just add a few charts to your report to jazz up presentation.

Here is a simple way to create a chart in Excel 2007.

1   Highlight the data area to be charted.
2   Go to "Insert" Tab.
3   Choose from "Charts": (e.g., "Pie").
4   The default data label is set on "Row" while the data value is on "Column". If your data is in column, use the "Switch Row/Column" button on the Data section.

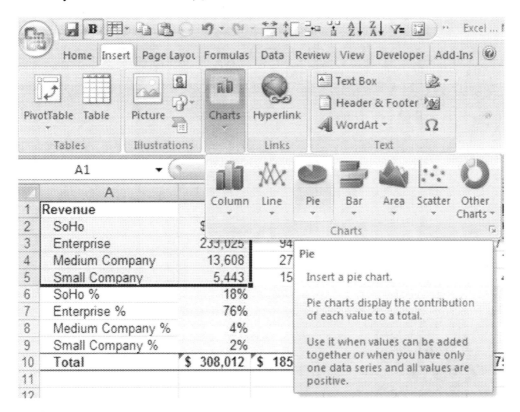

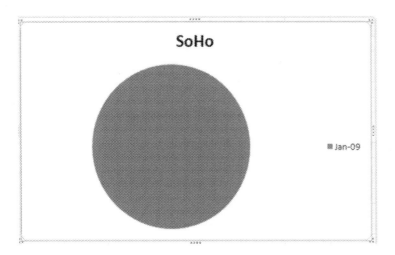

This is nice but it doesn't tell you anything...

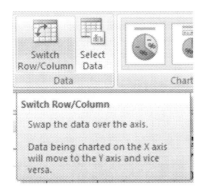

So you switch axis.

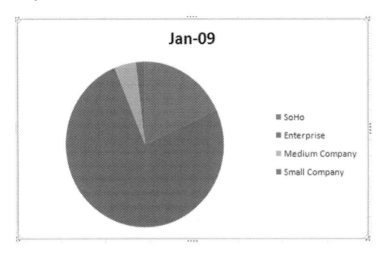

Steps in previous Excel versions

In previous version of Excel:

Highlight the data area to be charted.
"Insert" => "Chart"
Choose the type of chart. The example here is "Pie".
From "Data Range" choose column option if your data is top down.
From "Data Label" type in the appropriate description.
There are two options for the chart location.
    "New sheet option" - creates a new chart sheet.

    "Object In" - creates a chart within an existing worksheet.

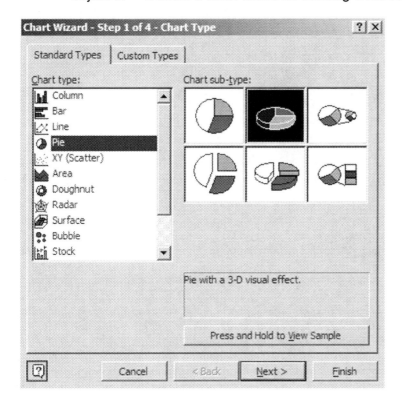

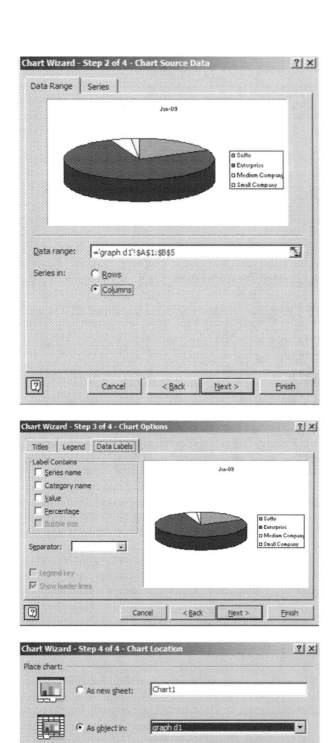

Two Axes graphs

You can graph two different types of values in one chart. For example, if you have values that are "Dollar" and "Percentage", you can use the "Line - Column on 2 axes" type of graph. Excel will automatically group similar value(s) together. I purposely started the example in the previous version of Excel because Excel 2007 is a bit complicated.

Steps in previous Excel versions

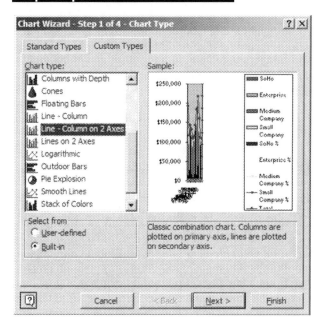

The sample below show left hand axes dollars in bars and right hand axes percentage in lines.

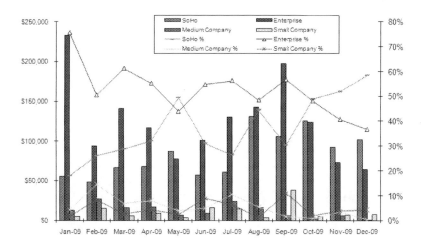

Steps in Excel 2007

Two axes graph in Excel 2007

Okay, I lied. It's really complicated to do it in Excel 2007. Follow the same steps as in making the pie chart above, but instead of choosing a pie chart, choose the "Column Chart".

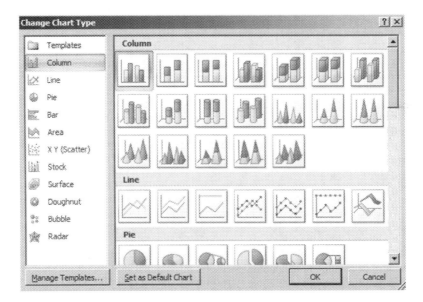

After you create a standard column bar chart, click on the chart which will prompt you to [Chart Tools].

From "Chart Tools" select [Layout] tab.

Select the percentage value from the drop down menu.

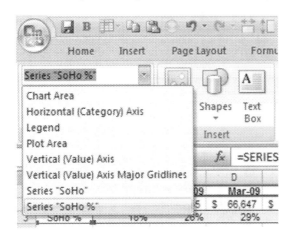

Select "Format" tab from "Chart Tools".

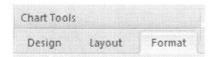

Press "Format Selection" then from "Format Data Series", click "Secondary Axis".

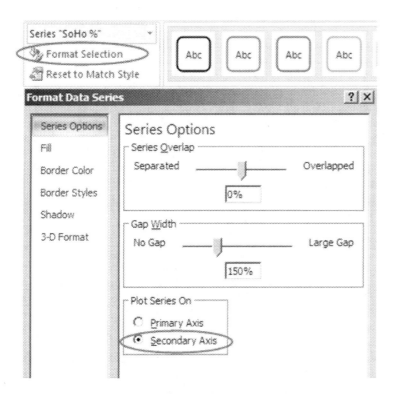

There should be two axis now: Left and Right.

Go to the "Design" tab.

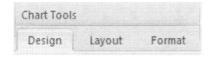

Choose "Change Chart Type".

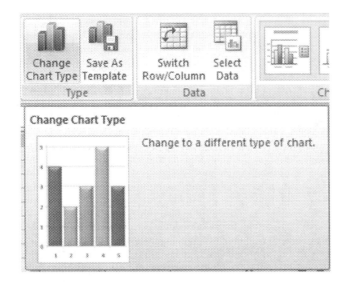

From "Change Series Chart Type"... and change the bar to "Line".

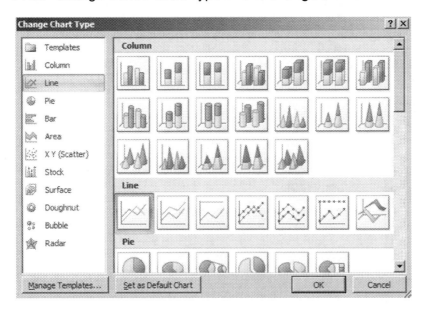

Unfortunately, if you have multiple series of percentages, this is a step you have to repeat for each series.

Use the older version of Excel and then open the file in Excel 2007. Excel is "usually" backward compatible.

Chapter 11: Creating Simple Marcos

Eliminate the monotony of doing the same thing over and over.

Macros

You can use macros to record repetitious actions and later recall them to automate certain tasks, all without learning the pesky VBA programming language!

Steps in Excel 2007

Marco is defaulted to disable status in Excel 2007 for security reasons. *If you enable macro, you could be increasing the chances of getting a computer virus. Wash your hands often, don't accept candy from strangers and most of all don't open Excel file from questionable sources.*

The steps below will show you how to activate and record simple macro.

Click on the Office Button

Go to "Excel Options"
From the "Popular" option check "Show Developer" tab in "Ribbon".
You will see a new tab or "Ribbon" – "Developer".
Click "Macro Security", and in "Macro Setting" click "Enable macro".

Recording a Macro

Click "Record Macro", and give it a name to start recording.
Your keystrokes will be converted to a macro and recorded until you press "Stop Recording".

Editing a Macro

Press Macro and choose Edit to bring up the VBA Module. You can review and edit the code directly from here. Try to experiment with recording different types of macros. You will soon understand the basic code, even if you are not a programmer.

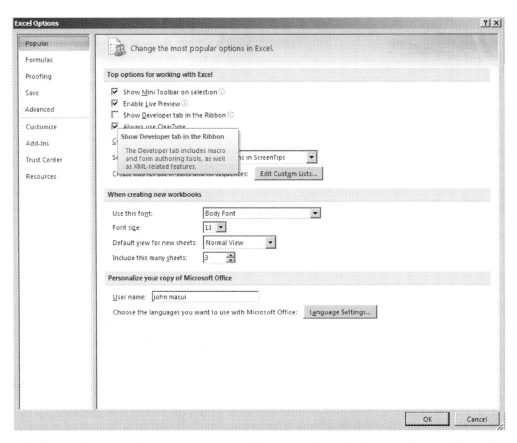

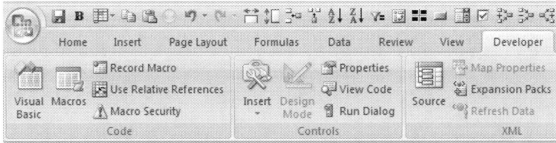

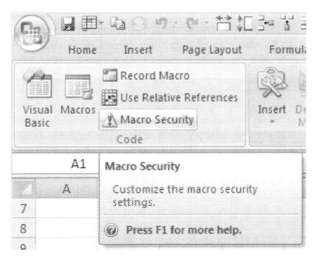

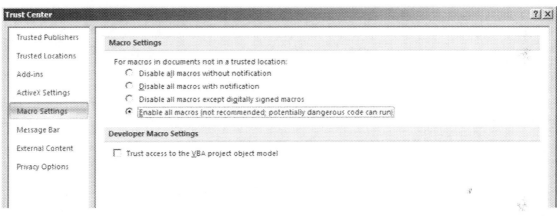

Steps in previous Excel versions

"Tools" => "Macro" => "Record New Macro".

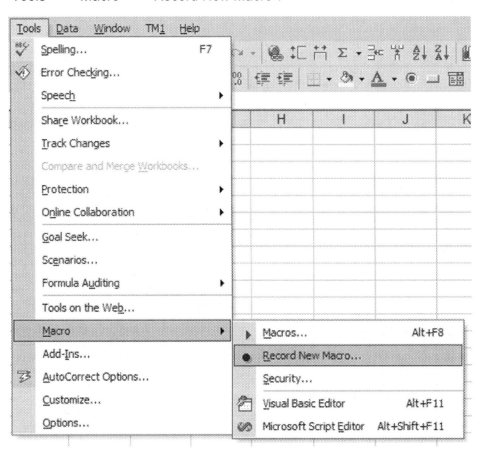

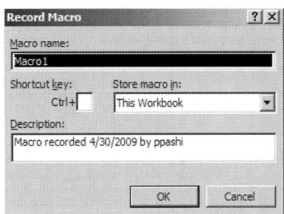

When macro recording is active, you will see this.

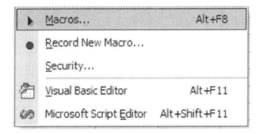

To end macro recording, press the square button.

To edit the macro "Tools" => "Macro" => "Macros".

VBA editor will be prompted.

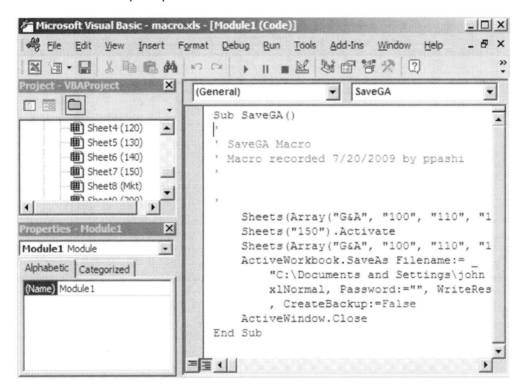

Applications

Suppose you are responsible for the overall department budget. You need to send the appropriate sections to each of the department managers whenever there are updates. "Macro" is perfect for these kinds of repetitive tasks.

Steps in Excel 2007

Choose "Record Macro" from the Developer tab.

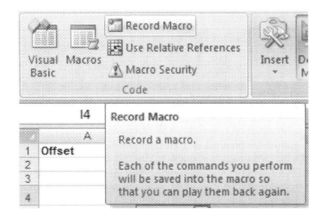

Highlight the section of sheets, for example all of G&A.

Right click and choose move or copy.

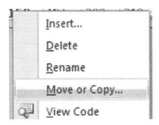

Choose "New Book".

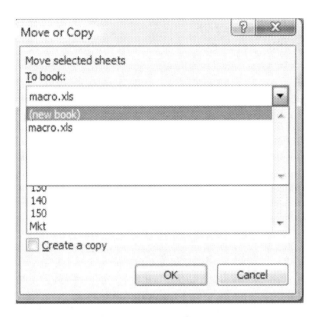

Save the new book as "G&A".
Stop recording.

You can really jazz it up by assigning a button to the macro. At the press of a button, you can run the macro.

> In Excel 2007, from the Developer ribbon choose "Insert".
> Choose "Button" (form control)
> Assign the macro name. You can always reassign the macro by right-clicking on the button and choosing some other macro .

Below is the VBA code that was recorded. The programming language is simple enough to guess at what the code is doing. By substituting the department numbers below you can save different compositions of cost centers.

```
Sub SaveGA()

'

' SaveGA Macro

' Macro recorded 7/20/2009 by xxx

'

'

    Sheets(Array("G&A", "100", "110", "120", "130", "140", "150")).Select

    Sheets("150").Activate

    Sheets(Array("G&A", "100", "110", "120", "130", "140", "150")).Copy

    ActiveWorkbook.SaveAs Filename:= _

        "C:\Documents and Settings\john masui\My Documents\G&A.xls", FileFormat:= _

        xlNormal, Password:="", WriteResPassword:="", ReadOnlyRecommended:=False _

        , CreateBackup:=False

    ActiveWindow.Close

End Sub
```

Index

#

A

C

D

F

G

H

I

Index